Sir Humphrey Gilbert's Voyage to Newfoundland

Edward Hayes

Contents

INTRODUCTORY NOTE 7
SIR HUMPHREY GILBERT'S VOYAGE TO NEWFOUNDLAND........................9

SIR HUMPHREY GILBERT'S VOYAGE TO NEWFOUNDLAND

BY

Edward Hayes

INTRODUCTORY NOTE

Sir Humphrey Gilbert, the founder of the first English colony in North America, was born about 1539, the son of a Devonshire gentleman, whose widow afterward married the father of Sir Walter Raleigh. He was educated at Eton and Oxford, served under Sir Philip Sidney's father in Ireland, and fought for the Netherlands against Spain. After his return he composed a pamphlet urging the search for a northwest passage to Cathay, which led to Frobisher's license for his explorations to that end.

In 1578 Gilbert obtained from Queen Elizabeth the charter he had long sought, to plant a colony in North America. His first attempt failed, and cost him his whole fortune; but, after further service in Ireland, he sailed again in 1583 for Newfoundland. In the August of that year he took possession of the harbor of St. John and founded his colony, but on the return voyage he went down with his ship in a storm south of the Azores.

The following narrative is an account of this last voyage of Gilbert's, told by Edward Hayes, commander of "The Golden Hind," the only one to reach England of the three ships which set out from Newfoundland with Gilbert.

The settlement at St. John was viewed by its promoter as merely the beginning of a scheme for ousting Spain from America in favor of

England. The plan did not progress as he hoped; but after long delays, and under far other impulses than Gilbert ever thought of, much of his dream was realized.

SIR HUMPHREY GILBERT'S VOYAGE TO NEWFOUNDLAND

A report of the Voyage and success thereof, attempted in the year of our Lord 1583, by Sir Humphrey Gilbert, Knight, with other gentlemen assisting him in that action, intended to discover and to plant Christian inhabitants in place convenient, upon those large and ample countries extended northward from the Cape of Florida, lying under very temperate climes, esteemed fertile and rich in minerals, yet not in the actual possession of any Christian prince. Written by Mr. Edward Hayes, gentleman, and principal actor in the same voyage,[1] who alone continued unto the end, and, by God's special assistance, returned home with his retinue safe and entire.

Many voyages have been pretended, yet hitherto never any thoroughly accomplished by our nation, of exact discovery into the bowels of those main, ample, and vast countries extended infinitely into the north from thirty degrees, or rather from twenty-five degrees, of septentrional latitude, neither hath a right way been taken of planting a Christian habitation and regiment (government) upon the same, as well may appear both by the little we yet do actually possess therein, and by our ignorance of the riches and secrets within those lands, which unto

---

1   Hayes was captain and owner of the ***Golden Hind***, Gilbert's Rear-Admiral.

this day we know chiefly by the travel and report of other nations, and most of the French, who albeit they cannot challenge such right and interest unto the said countries as we, neither these many years have had opportunity nor means so great to discover and to plant, being vexed with the calamities of intestine wars, as we have had by the inestimable benefit of our long and happy peace, yet have they both ways performed more, and had long since attained a sure possession and settled government of many provinces in those northerly parts of *America*, if their many attempts into those foreign and remote lands had not been impeached by their garboils at home.

The first discovery of these coasts, never heard of before, was well begun by John Cabot the father and Sebastian his son, an Englishman born, who were the first finders out of all that great tract of land stretching from the Cape of Florida, into those islands which we now call the Newfoundland; all which they brought and annexed unto the crown of England. Since when, if with like diligence the search of inland countries had been followed, as the discovery upon the coast and outparts thereof was performed by those two men, no doubt her Majesty's territories and revenue had been mightily enlarged and advanced by this day; and, which is more, the seed of Christian religion had been sowed amongst those pagans, which by this time might have brought forth a most plentiful harvest and copious congregation of Christians; which must be the chief intent of such as shall make any attempt that way; or else whatsoever is builded upon other foundation shall never obtain happy success nor continuance.

And although we cannot precisely judge (which only belongeth to God) what have been the humours of men stirred up to great attempts of discovering and planting in those remote countries, yet the events do shew that either God's cause hath not been chiefly preferred by them, or else God hath not permitted so abundant grace as the light of His word and knowledge of Him to be yet revealed unto those infidels before the appointed time. But most assuredly, the only cause of religion hitherto hath kept back, and will also bring forward at the time assigned by God, an effectual and complete discovery and possession by Christians both of those ample countries and the riches within them hitherto concealed; whereof, notwithstanding, God in His wisdom hath permitted to be revealed from time to time a certain obscure and misty knowledge, by little and little to allure the minds of men that way, which else will be dull enough in the zeal of His cause, and thereby to prepare us unto a readiness for the execution of His will, against the due time ordained of calling those pagans unto Christianity.

In the meanwhile it behoveth every man of great calling, in whom is any instinct of inclination unto this attempt, to examine his own motions, which, if the same proceed of ambition or avarice, he may assure himself it cometh not of God, and therefore cannot have confidence of God's protection and assistance against the violence (else irresistible) both of sea and infinite perils upon the land; whom God yet may use as an instrument to further His cause and glory some way, but not to build upon so bad a foundation. Otherwise, if his motives be derived from a virtuous and heroical mind, preferring chiefly the honour of God, compassion of poor infidels captived by the devil, tyrannizing in most wonderful and dreadful manner over their bodies and souls; advancement of his honest and well-disposed countrymen, willing to accompany him in such honourable actions; relief of sundry people within this realm distressed; all these be honourable purposes, imitating the nature of the munificent God, wherewith He is well pleased, who will assist such an actor beyond expectation of many. And the same, who feeleth this inclination in himself, by all likelihood may hope or rather confidently repose in the preordinance of God, that in this last age of the world (or likely never) the time is complete of receiving also these gentiles into His mercy, and that God will raise Him an instrument to effect the same; it seeming probable by event of precedent attempts made by the Spaniards and French sundry times, that the countries lying north of Florida God hath reserved the same to be reduced into Christian civility by the English nation. For not long after that Christopher Columbus had discovered the islands and continent of the West Indies for Spain, John and Sebastian Cabot made discovery also of the rest from Florida northwards to the behoof of England.

And whensoever afterwards the Spaniards, very prosperous in all their southern discoveries, did attempt anything into Florida and those regions inclining towards the north, they proved most unhappy, and were at length discouraged utterly by the hard and lamentable success of many both religious and valiant in arms, endeavouring to bring those northerly regions also under the Spanish jurisdiction, as if God had prescribed limits unto the Spanish nation which they might not exceed; as by their own gests recorded may be aptly gathered.

The French, as they can pretend less title unto these northern parts than the Spaniard, by how much the Spaniard made the first discovery of the same continent so far northward as unto Florida, and the French did but review that before discovered by the English nation, usurping upon our right, and imposing names upon countries, rivers, bays, capes, or headlands as if they had been the first finders of those coasts; which injury we offered not unto the Spaniards, but left off to discover when we approached the Spanish limits; even so God hath not hitherto permitted them to establish a possession permanent upon another's right, notwithstanding their manifold attempts, in which the issue hath been no less tragical than that of the Spaniards, as by their own reports is extant.

Then, seeing the English nation only hath right unto these countries of America from the Cape of Florida northward by the privilege of first discovery, unto which Cabot was authorised by regal authority, and set forth by the expense of our late famous King Henry the Seventh; which right also seemeth strongly defended on our behalf by the powerful hand of Almighty God withstanding the enterprises of other nations; it may greatly encourage us upon so just ground, as is our right, and upon so sacred an intent, as to plant religion (our right and intent being meet foundations for the same), to prosecute effectually the full possession of those so ample and pleasant countries appertaining unto the crown of England; the same, as is to be conjectured by infallible arguments of the world's end approaching, being now arrived unto the time of God prescribed of their vocation, if ever their calling unto the knowledge of God may be expected. Which also is very probable by the revolution and course of God's word and religion, which from the beginning hath moved from the east towards, and at last unto, the west, where it is like to end, unless the same begin again where it did in the east, which were to expect a like world again. But we are assured of the contrary by the prophecy of Christ, whereby we gather that after His word preached throughout the world shall be the end. And as the Gospel when it descended westward began in the south, and afterward begun in the south countries of America, no less hope may be gathered that it will also spread into the north.

These considerations may help to suppress all dreads rising of hard events in attempts made this way by other nations, as also of the heavy success and issue in the late enterprise made by a worthy gentleman our countryman, Sir Humfrey Gilbert, Knight, who was the first of our nations that carried people to erect an habitation and government in those northerly countries of America. About which albeit he had consumed much substance, and lost his life at last, his people also perishing for the most part: yet the mystery thereof we must leave unto God, and judge charitably both of the cause, which was just in all pretence, and of the person, who was very zealous in prosecuting the same, deserving honourable remembrance for his good mind and expense of life in so virtuous an enterprise. Whereby nevertheless, lest any man should be dismayed by example of other folks' calamity, and misdeem that God doth resist all attempts intended that way, I thought good, so far as myself was an eye-witness, to deliver the circumstance and manner of our proceedings in that action; in which the gentleman was so unfortunately encumbered with wants, and worse matched with many ill-disposed people, that his rare judgment and regiment premeditated for those affairs was subjected to tolerate abuses, and in sundry extremities to hold on a course more to uphold credit than likely in his own conceit happily to succeed.

The issue of such actions, being always miserable, not guided by God, who abhorreth confusion and disorder, hath left this for admonition, being the first attempt by our nation to plant, unto such as shall take the same cause in hand hereafter, not to be discouraged from it; but to make men well advised how they handle His so high and excellent matters, as the carriage is of His word into those very mighty and vast countries. An action doubtless not to be intermeddled with base purposes, as many have made the same but a colour to shadow actions otherwise scarce justifiable; which doth excite God's heavy judgments in the end, to the terrifying of weak minds from the cause, without pondering His just proceedings; and doth also incense foreign princes against our attempts, how just soever, who cannot but deem the sequel very dangerous unto their state (if in those parts we should grow to strength), seeing the very beginnings are entered with spoil.

And with this admonition denounced upon zeal towards God's cause, also towards those in whom appeareth disposition honourable unto this action of planting Christian people and religion in those remote and barbarous nations of America (unto whom I wish all happiness), I will now proceed to make relations briefly, yet particularly, of our voyage undertaken with Sir Humfrey Gilbert, begun, continued, and ended adversely.

When first Sir Humfrey Gilbert undertook the western discovery of America, and had procured from her Majesty a very large commission to inhabit and possess at his choice all remote and heathen lands not in the actual possession of any Christian prince, the same commission exemplified with many privileges, such as in his discretion he might demand, very many gentlemen of good estimation drew unto him, to associate him in so commendable an enterprise, so that the preparation was expected to grow unto a puissant fleet, able to encounter a king's power by sea. Nevertheless, amongst a multitude of voluntary men, their dispositions were diverse, which bred a jar, and made a division in the end, to the confusion of that attempt even before the same was begun. And when the shipping was in a manner prepared, and men ready upon the coast to go aboard, at that time some brake consort, and followed courses degenerating from the voyage before pretended. Others failed of their promises contracted, and the greater number were dispersed, leaving the General with few of his assured friends, with whom he adventured to sea; where, having tasted of no less misfortune, he was shortly driven to retire home with the loss of a tall ship and, more to his grief, of a valiant gentleman, Miles Morgan.

Having buried, only in a preparation, a great mass of substance, whereby his estate was impaired, his mind yet not dismayed, he continued his former designment, and purposed to revive this enterprise, good occasion serving. Upon which determination standing long without means to satisfy his desire, at last he granted certain assignments out of his commission to sundry persons of mean ability, desiring the privilege of his grant, to plant and fortify in the north parts of America about the river of Canada; to whom if God gave good success in the north parts (where then no matter of moment was expected), the same, he thought, would greatly advance the hope of the south, and be a furtherance unto his determination that way. And the worst that might happen in that course might be excused, without prejudice unto him, by the former supposition that those north regions were of no regard. But chiefly, a possession taken in any parcel of those heathen countries, by virtue of his grant, did invest him of territories extending every way 200 leagues; which induced Sir Humfrey Gilbert to make those assignments, desiring greatly their expedition, because his commission did expire after six years, if in that space he had not gotten actual possession.

Time went away without anything done by his assigns; insomuch that at last he must resolve himself to take a voyage in person, for more assurance to keep his patent in force, which then almost was expired or within two years. In furtherance of his determination, amongst others, Sir George Peckham, Knight, shewed himself very zealous to the action, greatly aiding him both by his advice and in the charge. Other gentlemen to their ability joined unto him, resolving to adventure their substance and lives in the same cause. Who beginning their preparation from that time, both of shipping, munition, victual, men, and things requisite, some of them continued the charge two years complete without intermission. Such were the difficulties and cross accidents opposing these proceedings, which took not end in less than two years; many of which circumstances I will omit.

The last place of our assembly, before we left the coast of England, was in Cawset Bay, near unto Plymouth, then resolved to put unto the sea with shipping and provision such as we had, before our store yet remaining, but chiefly the time and season of the year, were too far spent. Nevertheless, it seemed first very doubtful by what way to shape our course, and to begin our intended discovery, either from the south northward or from the north southward. The first, that is, beginning south, without all controversy was the likeliest, wherein we were assured to have commodity of the current which from the Cape of Florida setteth northward, and would have furthered greatly our navigation, discovering from the foresaid cape along towards Cape Breton, and all those lands lying to the north. Also, the year being far spent, and arrived to the month of June, we were not to spend time in northerly courses, where we should be surprised with timely winter, but to covet the south, which we had space enough then to have attained, and there might with less detriment have wintered that season, being more mild and short in the south than in the north, where winter is both long and rigorous. These and other like reasons alleged in favour of the southern course first to be taken, to the contrary was inferred that forasmuch as both our victuals and many other needful provisions were diminished and left insufficient for so long a voyage and for the wintering of so many men, we ought to shape a course most likely to minister supply; and that was to take the Newfoundland in our way, which was but 700 leagues from our English coast. Where being usually at that time of the year, and until the fine of August, a multitude of ships repairing thither for fish, we should be relieved abundantly with many necessaries, which, after the fishing ended, they might well spare and freely impart unto us. Not staying long upon that Newland coast, we might proceed southward, and follow still the sun, until we arrived at places more temperate to our content.

By which reasons we were the rather induced to follow this northerly course, obeying unto necessity, which must be supplied. Otherwise, we doubted that sudden approach of winter, bringing with it continual fog and thick mists, tempest and rage of weather, also contrariety of currents descending from the Cape of Florida unto Cape Breton and Cape Race, would fall out to be great and irresistible impediments unto our further proceeding for that year, and compel us to winter in those north and cold regions. Wherefore, suppressing all objections to the contrary, we resolved to begin our course northward, and to follow, directly as we might, the trade way unto Newfoundland; from whence, after our refreshing and reparation of wants, we intended without delay, by God's permission, to proceed into the south, not omitting any river or bay which in all that large tract of land appeared to our view worthy of search. Immediately we agreed upon the manner of our course and orders to be observed in our voyage; which were delivered in writing, unto the captains and masters of every ship a copy, in manner following.

Every ship had delivered two bullets or scrolls, the one sealed up in wax, the other left open; in both which were included several watchwords. That open, serving upon our own coast or the coast of Ireland; the other sealed, was promised on all hands not to be broken up until we should be clear of the Irish coast; which from thenceforth did serve until we arrived and met all together in such harbours of the Newfoundland as were agreed for our rendezvous. The said watchwords being requisite to know our consorts whensoever by night, either by fortune of weather, our fleet dispersed should come together again; or one should hail another; or if by ill watch and steerage one ship should chance to fall aboard of another in the dark.

The reason of the bullet sealed was to keep secret that watchword while we were upon our own coast, lest any of the company stealing from the fleet might bewray the same; which known to an enemy, he might board us by night without mistrust, having our own watchword.

Orders agreed upon by the Captains and Masters to be observed by the fleet of Sir Humfrey Gilbert.

First, The Admiral to carry his flag by day, and his light by night.

2. Item, if the Admiral shall shorten his sail by night, then to shew two lights until he be answered again by every ship shewing one light for a short time.

3. Item, if the Admiral after his shortening of sail, as aforesaid, shall make more sail again; then he to shew three lights one above another.

4. Item, if the Admiral shall happen to hull in the night, then to make a wavering light over his other light, wavering the light upon a pole.

5. Item, if the fleet should happen to be scattered by weather, or other mishap, then so soon as one shall descry another, to hoise both topsails twice, if the weather will serve, and to strike them twice again; but if the weather serve not, then to hoise the maintopsail twice, and forthwith to strike it twice again.

6. Item, if it shall happen a great fog to fall, then presently every ship to bear up with the Admiral, if there be wind; but if it be a calm, then every ship to hull, and so to lie at hull till it clear. And if the fog do continue long, then the Admiral to shoot off two pieces every evening, and every ship to answer it with one shot; and every man bearing to the ship that is to leeward so near as he may.

7. Item, every master to give charge unto the watch to look out well, for laying aboard one of another in the night, and in fogs.

8. Item, every evening every ship to hail the Admiral, and so to fall astern him, sailing through the ocean; and being on the coast, every ship to hail him both morning and evening.

9. Item, if any ship be in danger in any way, by leak or otherwise, then she to shoot off a piece, and presently to bring out one light; whereupon every man to bear towards her, answering her with one light for a short time, and so to put it out again; thereby to give knowledge that they have seen her token.

10. Item, whensoever the Admiral shall hang out her ensign in the main shrouds, then every man to come aboard her as a token of counsel.

11. Item, if there happen any storm or contrary wind to the fleet after the discovery, whereby they are separated; then every ship to repair unto their last good port, there to meet again.

OUR COURSE *agreed upon*.

The course first to be taken for the discovery is to bear directly to Cape Race, the most southerly cape of Newfoundland; and there to harbour ourselves either in Rogneux or Fermous, being the first places appointed for our rendezvous, and the next harbours unto the northward of Cape Race: and therefore every ship separated from the fleet to repair to that place so fast as God shall permit, whether you shall fall to the southward or to the northward of it, and there to stay for the meeting of the whole fleet the space of ten days; and when you shall depart, to leave marks.

Beginning our course from Scilly, the nearest is by west-south-west (if the wind serve) until such time as we have brought ourselves in the latitude of 43 or 44 degrees, because the ocean is subject much to southerly winds in June and July. Then to take traverse from 45 to 47 degrees of latitude, if we be enforced by contrary winds; and not to go to the northward of the height of 47 degrees of septentrional latitude by no means, if God shall not enforce the contrary; but to do your endeavour to keep in the height of 46 degrees, so near as you can possibly, because Cape Race lieth about that height.

NOTE.

If by contrary winds we be driven back upon the coast of England, then to repair unto Scilly for a place of our assembly or meeting. If we be driven back by contrary winds that we cannot pass the coast of Ireland, then the place of our assembly to be at Bere haven or Baltimore haven. If we shall not happen to meet at Cape Race, then the place of rendezvous to be at Cape Breton, or the nearest harbour unto the westward of Cape Breton. If by means of other shipping we may not safely stay there, then to rest at the very next safe port to the westward; every ship leaving their marks behind them for the more certainty of the after comers to know where to find them. The marks that every man ought to leave in such a case, were of the General's private device written by himself, sealed also in close wax, and delivered unto every ship one scroll, which was not to be opened until occasion required, whereby every man was certified what to leave for instruction of after comers; that every of us coming into any harbour or river might know who had been there, or whether any were still there up higher into the river, or departed, and which way.

Orders thus determined, and promises mutually given to be observed, every man withdrew himself unto his charge; the anchors being already weighed, and our ships under sail, having a soft gale of wind, we began our voyage upon Tuesday, the 11 day of June, in the year of our Lord 1583, having in our fleet (at our departure from Cawset Bay) these ships, whose names and burthens, with the names of the captains and masters of them, I have also inserted, as followeth:--1. The *Delight*, alias the *George*, of burthen 120 tons, was Admiral; in which went the General, and William Winter, captain in her and part owner, and Richard Clarke, master. 2. The bark *Raleigh*, set forth by Master Walter Raleigh, of the burthen of 200 tons, was then Vice-Admiral; in which went Master Butler, captain, and Robert Davis, of Bristol, master. 3. The *Golden Hind*, of burthen 40 tons, was then Rear-Admiral; in which went Edward Hayes, captain and owner, and William Cox, of Limehouse, master. 4. The *Swallow*, of burthen 40 tons; in her was captain Maurice Browne. 5. The *Squirrel*, of burthen 10 tons; in which went captain William Andrews, and one Cade, master. We were in number in all about 260 men; among whom we had of every faculty good choice, as shipwrights, masons, carpenters, smiths, and such like, requisite to such an action; also mineral men and refiners. Besides, for solace of our people, and allurement of the savages, we were provided of music in good variety; not omitting the least toys, as morris-dancers, hobbyhorse, and May-like conceits to delight the savage people, whom we intended to win by all fair means possible. And to that end we were indifferently furnished of all petty haberdashery wares to barter with those simple people.

In this manner we set forward, departing (as hath been said) out of Cawset Bay the 11 day of June, being Tuesday, the weather and wind fair and good all day; but a great storm of thunder and wind fell the same night. Thursday following, when we hailed one another in the evening, according to the order before specified, they signified unto us out of the Vice-Admiral, that both the captain, and very many of the men, were fallen sick. And about midnight the Vice-Admiral forsook us, notwithstanding we had the wind east, fair and good. But it was after credibly reported that they were infected with a contagious sickness, and arrived greatly distressed at Plymouth; the reason I could never understand. Sure I am, no cost was spared by their owner, Master Raleigh, in setting them forth; therefore I leave it unto God. By this time we were in 48 degrees of latitude, not a little grieved with the loss of the most puissant ship in our fleet; after whose departure the *Golden Hind* succeeded in the place of Vice-Admiral, and removed her flag from the mizen into the foretop. From Saturday, the 15 of June, until the 28, which was upon a Friday, we never had fair day without fog or rain, and winds bad, much to the west-north-west, whereby we were driven southward unto 41 degrees scarce.

About this time of the year the winds are commonly west towards the Newfoundland, keeping ordinarily within two points of west to the south or to the north; whereby the course thither falleth out to be long and tedious after June, which in March, April, and May, hath been performed out of England in 22 days and less. We had wind always so scant from the west-north-west, and from west-south-west again, that our traverse was great, running south unto 41 degrees almost, and afterwards north into 51 degrees. Also we were encumbered with much fog and mists in manner palpable, in which we could not keep so well together, but were discovered, losing the company of the *Swallow* and the *Squirrel* upon the 20 day of July, whom we met again at several places upon the Newfoundland coast the 3 of August, as shall be declared in place convenient. Saturday, the 27 July, we might descry, not far from us, as it were mountains of ice driven upon the sea, being then in 50 degrees, which were carried southward to the weather of us; whereby may be conjectured that some current doth set that way from the north.

Before we came to Newfoundland, about 50 leagues on this side, we pass the bank, which are high grounds rising within the sea and under water, yet deep enough and without danger, being commonly not less than 25 and 30 fathom water upon them; the same, as it were some vein of mountains within the sea, do run along and form the Newfoundland, beginning northward about 52 or 53 degrees of latitude, and do extend into the south infinitely. The breadth of this bank is somewhere more, and somewhere less; but we found the same about ten leagues over, having sounded both on this side thereof, and the other toward Newfoundland, but found no ground with almost 200 fathom of line, both before and after we had passed the bank. The Portugals, and French chiefly, have a notable trade of fishing upon this bank, where are sometimes an hundred or more sails of ships, who commonly begin the fishing in April, and have ended by July. That fish is large, always wet, having no land near to dry, and is called cod fish. During the time of fishing, a man shall know without sounding when he is upon the bank, by the incredible multitude of sea-fowl hovering over the same, to prey upon the offals and garbage of fish thrown out by fishermen, and floating upon the sea.

Upon Tuesday, the 11 of June we forsook the coast of England. So again on Tuesday, the 30 of July, seven weeks after, we got sight of land, being immediately embayed in the Grand Bay, or some other great bay; the certainty whereof we could not judge, so great haze and fog did hang upon the coast, as neither we might discern the land well, nor take the sun's height. But by our best computation we were then in the 51 degrees of latitude. Forsaking this bay and uncomfortable coast (nothing appearing unto us but hideous rocks and mountains, bare of trees, and void of any green herb) we followed the coast to the south, with weather fair and clear. We had sight of an island named Penguin, of a fowl there breeding in abundance almost incredible, which cannot fly, their wings not able to carry their body, being very large (not much less than a goose) and exceeding fat, which the Frenchmen use to take without difficulty upon that island, and to barrel them up with salt. But for lingering of time, we had made us there the like provision.

Trending this coast, we came to the island called Baccalaos, being not past two leagues from the main; to the north thereof lieth Cape St. Francis, five leagues distant from Baccalaos, between which goeth in a great bay, by the vulgar sort called the Bay of Conception. Here we met with the *Swallow* again, whom we had lost in the fog, and all her men altered into other apparel; whereof it seemed their store was so amended, that for joy and congratulation of our meeting, they spared not to cast up into the air and overboard their caps and hats in good plenty. The captain, albeit himself was very honest and religious, yet was he not appointed of men to his humour and desert; who for the most part were such as had been by us surprised upon the narrow seas of England, being pirates, and had taken at that instant certain Frenchmen laden, one bark with wines, and another with salt. Both which we rescued, and took the man-of-war with all her men, which was the same ship now called the *Swallow*; following still their kind so oft as, being separated from the General, they found opportunity to rob and spoil. And because God's justice did follow the same company, even to destruction, and to the overthrow also of the captain (though not consenting to their misdemeanour) I will not conceal anything that maketh to the manifestation and approbation of His judgments, for examples of others; persuaded that God more sharply took revenge upon them, and hath tolerated longer as great outrage in others, by how much these went under protection of His cause and religion, which was then pretended.

Therefore upon further enquiry it was known how this company met with a bark returning home after the fishing with his freight; and because the men in the *Swallow* were very near scanted of victuals, and chiefly of apparel, doubtful withal where or when to find and meet with their Admiral, they besought the captain that they might go aboard this *Newlander*, only to borrow what might be spared, the rather because the same was bound homeward. Leave given, not without charge to deal favourably, they came aboard the fisherman, whom they rifled of tackle, sails, cables, victuals, and the men of their apparel; not sparing by torture, winding cords about their heads, to draw out else what they thought good. This done with expedition, like men skilful in such mischief, as they took their cockboat to go aboard their own ship, it was overwhelmed in the sea, and certain of these men there drowned; the rest were preserved even by those silly souls whom they had before spoiled, who saved and delivered them aboard the *Swallow*. What became afterwards of the poor *Newlander*, perhaps destitute of sails and furniture sufficient to carry them home, whither they had not less to run than 700 leagues, God alone knoweth; who took vengeance not long after of the rest that escaped at this instant, to reveal the fact, and justify to the world God's judgments indicted upon them, as shall be declared in place convenient.

Thus after we had met with the *Swallow*, we held on our course southward, until we came against the harbour called St. John, about five leagues from the former Cape of St. Francis, where before the entrance into the harbour, we found also the frigate or *Squirrel* lying at anchor; whom the English merchants, that were and always be Admirals by turns interchangeably over the fleets of fishermen within the same harbour, would not permit to enter into the harbour. Glad of so happy meeting, both of the *Swallow* and frigate in one day, being Saturday, the third of August, we made ready our fights, and prepared to enter the harbour, any resistance to the contrary notwithstanding, there being within of all nations to the number of 36 sails. But first the General despatched a boat to give them knowledge of his coming for no ill intent, having commission from her Majesty for his voyage he had in hand; and immediately we followed with a slack gale, and in the very entrance, which is but narrow, not above two butts' length, the Admiral fell upon a rock on the larboard side by great oversight, in that the weather was fair, the rock much above water fast by the shore, where neither went any sea-gate. But we found such readiness in the English merchants to help us in that danger, that without delay there were brought a number of boats, which towed off the ship, and cleared her of danger.

Having taken place convenient in the road, we let fall anchors, the captains and masters repairing aboard our Admiral; whither also came immediately the masters and owners of the fishing fleet of Englishmen, to understand the General's intent and cause of our arrival there. They were all satisfied when the General had shewed his commission and purpose to take possession of those lands to the behalf of the crown of England, and the advancement of the Christian religion in those paganish regions, requiring but their lawful aid for repairing of his fleet, and supply of some necessaries, so far as conveniently might be afforded him, both out of that and other harbours adjoining. In lieu whereof he made offer to gratify them with any favour and privilege, which upon their better advice they should demand, the like being not to be obtained hereafter for greater price. So craving expedition of his demand, minding to proceed further south without long detention in those parts, he dismissed them, after promise given of their best endeavour to satisfy speedily his so reasonable request. The merchants with their masters departed, they caused forthwith to be discharged all the great ordnance of their fleet in token of our welcome.

It was further determined that every ship of our fleet should deliver unto the merchants and masters of that harbour a note of all their wants:

which done, the ships, as well English as strangers, were taxed at an easy rate to make supply. And besides, commissioners were appointed, part of our own company and part of theirs, to go into other harbours adjoining (for our English merchants command all there) to levy our provision: whereunto the Portugals, above other nations, did most willingly and liberally contribute. In so much as we were presented, above our allowance, with wines, marmalades, most fine rusk or biscuit, sweet oils, and sundry delicacies. Also we wanted not of fresh salmons, trouts, lobsters, and other fresh fish brought daily unto us. Moreover as the manner is in their fishing, every week to choose their Admiral anew, or rather they succeed in orderly course, and have weekly their Admiral's feast solemnized: even so the General, captains, and masters of our fleet were continually invited and feasted. To grow short in our abundance at home the entertainment had been delightful; but after our wants and tedious passage through the ocean, it seemed more acceptable and of greater contentation, by how much the same was unexpected in that desolate corner of the world; where, at other times of the year, wild beasts and birds have only the fruition of all those countries, which now seemed a place very populous and much frequented.

The next morning being Sunday, and the fourth of August, the General and his company were brought on land by English merchants, who shewed unto us their accustomed walks unto a place they call the Garden. But nothing appeared more than nature itself without art: who confusedly hath brought forth roses abundantly, wild, but odoriferous, and to sense very comfortable. Also the like plenty of raspberries, which do grow in every place.

Monday following, the General had his tent set up; who, being accompanied with his own followers, summoned the merchants and masters, both English and strangers, to be present at his taking possession of those countries. Before whom openly was read, and interpreted unto the strangers, his commission: by virtue whereof he took possession in the same harbour of St. John, and 200 leagues every way, invested the Queen's Majesty with the title and dignity thereof, had delivered unto him, after the custom of England, a rod, and a turf of the same soil, entering possession also for him, his heirs and assigns for ever; and signified unto all men, that from that time forward, they should take the same land as a territory appertaining to the Queen of England, and himself authorised under her Majesty to possess and enjoy it, and to ordain laws for the government thereof, agreeable, so near as conveniently might be, unto the laws of England, under which all people coming thither hereafter, either to inhabit, or by way of traffic, should be subjected and governed. And especially at the same time for a beginning, he proposed and delivered three laws to be in force immediately. That is to say the first for religion, which in public exercise should be according to the Church of England. The second, for maintenance of her Majesty's right and possession of those territories, against which if any thing were attempted prejudicial, the party or parties offending should be adjudged and executed as in case of high treason, according to the laws of England. The third, if any person should utter words sounding to the dishonour of her Majesty, he should lose his ears, and have his ship and goods confiscate.

These contents published, obedience was promised by general voice and consent of the multitude, as well of Englishmen as strangers, praying for continuance of this possession and government begun; after this, the assembly was dismissed. And afterwards were erected not far from that place the arms of England engraven in lead, and infixed upon a pillar of wood. Yet further and actually to establish this possession taken in the right of her Majesty, and to the behoof of Sir Humfrey Gilbert, knight, his heirs and assigns for ever, the General granted in fee-farm divers parcels of land lying by the water-side, both in this harbour of St. John, and elsewhere, which was to the owners a great commodity, being thereby assured, by their proper inheritance, of grounds convenient to dress and to dry their fish; whereof many times before they did fail, being prevented by them that came first into the harbour. For which grounds they did covenant to pay a certain rent and service unto Sir Humfrey Gilbert, his heirs or assigns for ever, and yearly to maintain possession of the same, by themselves or their assigns.

Now remained only to take in provision granted, according as every ship was taxed, which did fish upon the coast adjoining. In the meanwhile, the General appointed men unto their charge: some to repair and trim the ships, others to attend in gathering together our supply and provisions: others to search the commodities and singularities of the country, to be found by sea or land, and to make relation unto the General what either themselves could know by their own travail and experience, or by good intelligence of Englishmen or strangers, who had longest frequented the same coast. Also some observed the elevation of the pole, and drew plots of the country exactly graded. And by that I could gather by each man's several relation, I have drawn a brief description of the Newfoundland, with the commodities by sea or land already made, and such also as are in possibility and great likelihood to be made. Nevertheless the cards and plots that were drawn, with the due gradation of the harbours, bays, and capes, did perish with the Admiral: wherefore in the description following, I must omit the particulars of such things.

That which we do call the Newfoundland, and the Frenchmen *Baccalaos*, is an island, or rather, after the opinion of some, it consisteth of sundry islands and broken lands, situate in the north regions of America, upon the gulf and entrance of a great river called St. Lawrence in Canada; into the which, navigation may be made both on the south and north side of this island. The land lieth south and north, containing in length between 300 and 400 miles, accounting from Cape Race, which is in 46 degrees 25 minutes, unto the Grand Bay in 52 degrees, of septentrional latitude. The land round about hath very many goodly bays and harbours, safe roads for ships, the like not to be found in any part of the known world.

The common opinion that is had of intemperature and extreme cold that should be in this country, as of some part it may be verified, namely the north, where I grant it is more cold than in countries of Europe, which are under the same elevation: even so it cannot stand with reason and nature of the clime, that the south parts should be so intemperate as the bruit hath gone. For as the same do lie under the climes of Bretagne, Anjou, Poictou in France, between 46 and 49 degrees, so can they not so much differ from the temperature of those countries: unless upon the out-coast lying open unto the ocean and sharp winds, it must indeed be subject to more cold than further within the land, where the mountains are interposed as walls and bulwarks, to defend and to resist the asperity and rigour of the sea and weather. Some hold opinion that the Newfoundland might be the more subject to cold, by how much it lieth high and near unto the middle region. I grant that not in Newfoundland alone, but in Germany, Italy and Afric, even under the equinoctial line, the mountains are extreme cold, and seldom uncovered of snow, in their culm and highest tops, which cometh to pass by the same reason that they are extended towards the middle region: yet in the countries lying beneath them, it is found quite contrary. Even so, all hills having their descents, the valleys also and low grounds must be likewise hot or temperate, as the clime doth give in Newfoundland: though I am of opinion that the sun's reflection is much cooled, and cannot be so forcible in Newfoundland, nor generally throughout America, as in Europe or Afric: by how much the sun in his diurnal course from east to west, passeth over, for the most part, dry land and sandy countries, before he arriveth at the west of Europe or Afric, whereby his motion increaseth heat, with little or no qualification by moist vapours. Whereas, on the contrary, he passeth from Europe and Afric unto American over the ocean, from whence he draweth and carrieth with him abundance of moist vapours, which do qualify and enfeeble greatly the sun's reverberation upon this country chiefly of Newfoundland, being so much to the northward. Nevertheless, as I said before, the cold cannot be so intolerable under the latitude of 46, 47, and 48, especial within land, that it should be unhabitable, as some do suppose, seeing also there are very many people more to the north by a great deal. And in these south parts there be certain beasts, ounces or leopards, and birds in like manner, which in the summer we have seen, not heard of in countries of extreme and vehement coldness. Besides, as in the months of June, July, August and September, the heat is somewhat more than in England at those seasons: so men remaining upon the south parts near unto Cape Race, until after holland-tide (All-hallow-tide--November 1), have not found the cold so extreme, nor much differing from the temperature of England. Those which have arrived there after November and December have found the snow exceeding deep, whereat no marvel, considering the ground upon the coast is rough and uneven, and the snow is driven into the places most declining, as the like is to be seen with us. The like depth of snow happily shall not be found within land upon the plainer countries, which also are defended by the mountains, breaking off the violence of winds and weather. But admitting extraordinary cold in those south parts, above that with us here, it cannot be so great as in

Swedeland, much less in Moscovia or Russia: yet are the same countries very populous, and the rigour of cold is dispensed with by the commodity of stoves, warm clothing, meats and drinks: all of which need not be wanting in the Newfoundland, if we had intent there to inhabit.

In the south parts we found no inhabitants, which by all likelihood have abandoned those coasts, the same being so much frequented by Christians; but in the north are savages altogether harmless. Touching the commodities of this country, serving either for sustentation of inhabitants or for maintenance of traffic, there are and may be made divers; so that it seemeth that nature hath recompensed that only defect and incommodity of some sharp cold, by many benefits; namely, with incredible quantity, and no less variety, of kinds of fish in the sea and fresh waters, as trouts, salmons, and other fish to us unknown; also cod, which alone draweth many nations thither, and is become the most famous fishing of the world; abundance of whales, for which also is a very great trade in the bays of Placentia and the Grand Bay, where is made train oil of the whale; herring, the largest that have been heard of, and exceeding the Marstrand herring of Norway; but hitherto was never benefit taken of the herring fishing. There are sundry other fish very delicate, namely, the bonito, lobsters, turbot, with others infinite not sought after; oysters having pearl but not orient in colour; I took it, by reason they were not gathered in season.

Concerning the inland commodities, as well to be drawn from this land, as from the exceeding large countries adjoining, there is nothing which our east and northerly countries of Europe do yield, but the like also may be made in them as plentifully, by time and industry; namely, resin, pitch, tar, soap-ashes, deal-board, masts for ships, hides, furs, flax, hemp, corn, cables, cordage, linen cloth, metals, and many more. All which the countries will afford, and the soil is apt to yield. The trees for the most in those south parts are fir-trees, pine, and cypress, all yielding gum and turpentine. Cherry trees bearing fruit no bigger than a small pease. Also pear-trees, but fruitless. Other trees of some sort to us unknown. The soil along the coast is not deep of earth, bringing forth abundantly peasen small, yet good feeding for cattle. Roses passing sweet, like unto our musk roses in form; raspises; a berry which we call whorts, good and wholesome to eat. The grass and herb doth fat sheep in very short space, proved by English merchants which have carried sheep thither for fresh victual and had them raised exceeding fat in less than three weeks. Peasen which our countrymen have sown in the time of May, have come up fair, and been gathered in the beginning of August, of which our General had a present acceptable for the rareness, being the first fruits coming up by art and industry in that desolate and dishabited land. Lakes or pools of fresh water, both on the tops of mountains and in the valleys; in which are said to be muscles not unlike to have pearl, which I had put in trial, if by mischance falling unto me I had not been letted from that and other good experiments I was minded to make. Fowl both of water and land in great plenty and diversity. All kind of green fowl; others as big as bustards, yet not the same. A great white fowl called of some a gaunt. Upon the land divers sort of hawks, as falcons, and others by report. Partridges most plentiful, larger than ours, grey and white of colour, and rough-footed like doves, which our men after one flight did kill with cudgels, they were so fat and unable to fly. Birds, some like blackbirds, linnets, canary birds, and other very small. Beasts of sundry kinds; red deer, buffles, or a beast as it seemeth by the tract and foot very large, in manner of an ox. Bears, ounces or leopards, some greater and some lesser; wolves, foxes, which to the northward a little farther are black, whose fur is esteemed in some countries of Europe very rich. Otters, beavers, marterns; and in the opinion of most men that saw it, the General had brought unto him a sable alive, which he sent unto his brother, Sir John Gilbert, Knight, of Devonshire, but it was never delivered, as after I understood. We could not observe the hundredth part of creatures in those unhabited lands; but these mentioned may induce us to glorify the magnificent God, who hath super-abundantly replenished the earth with creatures serving for the use of man, though man hath not used the fifth part of the same, which the more doth aggravate the fault and foolish sloth in many of our nations, choosing rather to live indirectly, and very miserably to live and die within this realm pestered with inhabitants, then to adventure as becometh men, to obtain an habitation in those remote lands, in which nature very prodigally doth minister unto men's endeavours, and for art to work upon. For besides these already recounted and infinite more, the mountains generally make shew of mineral substance; iron very common, lead, and somewhere copper. I will not aver of richer metals; albeit by the circumstances following, more than hope may be conceived thereof.

For amongst other charges given to enquire out the singularities of this country, the General was most curious in the search of metals, commanding the mineral-man and refiner especially to be diligent. The same was a Saxon born, honest, and religious, named Daniel. Who after search brought at first some sort of ore, seeming rather to be iron than other metal. The next time he found ore, which with no small show of contentment he delivered unto the General, using protestation that if silver were the thing which might satisfy the General and his followers, there it was, advising him to seek no further; the peril whereof he undertook upon his life (as dear unto him as the crown of England unto her Majesty, that I may use his own words) if it fell not out accordingly.

Myself at this instant liker to die than to live, by a mischance, could not follow this confident opinion of our refiner to my own satisfaction; but afterward demanding our General's opinion therein, and to have some part of the ore, he replied, *Content yourself, I have seen enough; and were it but to satisfy my private humour, I would proceed no further. The promise unto my friends, and necessity to bring also the south countries within compass of my patent near expired, as we have already done these north parts, do only persuade me further. And touching the ore, I have sent it aboard, whereof I would have no speech to be made so long as we remain within harbour; here being both Portugals, Biscayans, and Frenchmen, not far off, from whom must be kept any bruit or muttering of such matter. When we are at sea, proof shall be made; if it be our desire, we may return the sooner hither again.* Whose answer I judged reasonable, and contenting me well; wherewith I will conclude this narration and description of the Newfoundland, and proceed to the rest of our voyage, which ended tragically.

While the better sort of us were seriously occupied in repairing our wants, and contriving of matters for the commodity of our voyage, others of another sort and disposition were plotting of mischief; some casting to steal away our shipping by night, watching opportunity by the General's and captains' lying on the shore; whose conspiracies discovered, they were prevented. Others drew together in company, and carried away out of the harbours adjoining a ship laden with fish, setting the poor men on shore. A great many more of our people stole into the woods to hide themselves, attending time and means to return home by such shipping as daily departed from the coast. Some were sick of fluxes, and many dead; and in brief, by one means or other our company was diminished, and many by the General licensed to return home. Insomuch as after we had reviewed our people, resolved to see an end of our voyage, we grew scant of men to furnish all our shipping; it seemed good thereof unto the General to leave the *Swallow* with such provision as might be spared for transporting home the sick people.

The captain of the *Delight* or Admiral, returned into England, in whose stead was appointed captain Maurice Browne, before the captain of the *Swallow*; who also brought with him into the *Delight* all his men of the *Swallow*, which before have been noted of outrage perpetrated and committed upon fishermen there met at sea.

The General made choice to go in his frigate the *Squirrel*, whereof the captain also was amongst them that returned into England; the same frigate being most convenient to discover upon the coast, and to search into every harbour or creek, which a great ship could not do. Therefore the frigate was prepared with her nettings and fights, and overcharged with bases and such small ordnance, more to give a show, than with judgment to foresee unto the safety of her and the men, which afterward was an occasion also of their overthrow.

Now having made ready our shipping, that is to say, the *Delight*, the *Golden Hind*, and the *Squirrel*, we put aboard our provision, which was wines, bread or rusk, fish wet and dry, sweet oils, besides many other, as marmalades, figs, limons barrelled, and such like. Also we had other necessary provision for trimming our ships, nets and lines to fish withal, boats or pinnaces fit for discovery. In brief, we were supplied of our wants commodiously, as if we had been in a country or some city populous and plentiful of all things.

We departed from this harbour of St. John's upon Tuesday, the 20 of August, which we found by exact observation to be in 47 degrees 40 minutes; and the next day by night we were at Cape Race, 25 leagues from the same harborough. This cape lieth south-south-west from St. John's; it is a low land, being off from the cape about half a league; within the sea riseth up a rock against the point of the cape, which thereby is easily known. It is in latitude 46 degrees 25 minutes. Under this cape we were becalmed a small time, during which we laid out hooks and lines to take cod, and drew in less than two hours fish so large and in such abundance, that many days after we fed upon no other provision. From hence we shaped our course unto the island of Sablon, if conveniently it would so fall out, also directly to Cape Breton.

Sablon lieth to the seaward of Cape Breton about 25 leagues, whither we were determined to go upon intelligence we had of a Portugal, during our abode in St. John's, who was himself present when the Portugals, above thirty years past, did put into the same island both neat and swine to breed, which were since exceedingly multiplied. This seemed unto us very happy tidings, to have in an island lying so near unto the main, which we intended to plant upon, such store of cattle, whereby we might at all times conveniently be relieved of victual, and served of store for breed.

In this course we trended along the coast, which from Cape Race stretcheth into the north-west, making a bay which some called Trepassa. Then it goeth out again towards the west, and maketh a point, which with Cape Race lieth in manner east and west. But this point inclineth to the north, to the west of which goeth in the Bay of Placentia. We sent men on land to take view of the soil along this coast, whereof they made good report, and some of them had will to be planted there. They saw pease growing in great abundance everywhere.

The distance between Cape Race and Cape Breton is 87 leagues; in which navigation we spent eight days, having many times the wind indifferent good, yet could we never attain sight of any land all that time, seeing we were hindered by the current. At last we fell into such flats and dangers that hardly any of us escaped; where nevertheless we lost our Admiral (the *Delight*) with all the men and provisions, not knowing certainly the place. Yet for inducing men of skill to make conjecture, by our course and way we held from Cape Race thither, that thereby the flats and dangers may be inserted in sea cards, for warning to others that may follow the same course hereafter, I have set down the best reckonings that were kept by expert men, William Cox, Master of the *Hind*, and John Paul, his mate, both of Limehouse. . . . Our course we held in clearing us of these flats was east-south-east, and south-east, and south, fourteen leagues, with a marvellous scant wind.

Upon Tuesday, the 27 of August, toward the evening, our General caused them in his frigate to sound, who found white sand at 35 fathom, being then in latitude about 44 degrees. Wednesday, toward night, the wind came south, and we bare with the land all that night, west-north-west, contrary to the mind of Master Cox; nevertheless we followed the Admiral, deprived of power to prevent a mischief, which by no contradiction could be brought to hold another course, alleging they could not make the ship to work better, nor to lie otherways. The evening was fair and pleasant, yet not without token of storm to ensue, and most part of this Wednesday night, like the swan that singeth before her death, they in the Admiral, or *Delight*, continued in sounding of trumpets, with drums and fifes; also winding the cornets and hautboys, and in the end of their jollity, left with the battle and ringing of doleful knells. Towards the evening also we caught in the *Golden Hind* a very mighty porpoise with harping iron, having first stricken divers of them, and brought away part of their flesh sticking upon the iron, but could recover only that one. These also, passing through the ocean in herds, did portend storm. I omit to recite frivolous report by them in the frigate, of strange voices the same night, which scared some from the helm.

Thursday, the 29 of August, the wind rose, and blew vehemently at south and by east, bringing withal rain and thick mist, so that we could not see a cable length before us; and betimes in the morning we were altogether run and folded in amongst flats and sands, amongst which we found shoal and deep in every three or four ships' length, after we began to sound; but first we were upon them unawares, until Master Cox looking out, discerned, in his judgment, white cliffs, crying **Land!** withal; though we could not afterward descry any land, it being very likely the breaking of the sea white, which seemed to be white cliffs, through the haze and thick weather.

Immediately tokens were given unto the ***Delight***, to cast about to seaward, which, being the greater ship, and of burthen 120 tons, was yet foremost upon the breach, keeping so ill watch, that they knew not the danger, before they felt the same, too late to recover it; for presently the Admiral struck aground, and has soon after her stern and hinder parts beaten in pieces; whereupon the rest (that is to say, the frigate, in which was the General, and the ***Golden Hind***) cast about east-southeast, bearing to the south, even for our lives, into the wind's eye, because that way carried us to the seaward. Making out from this danger, we sounded one while seven fathom, then five fathom, then four fathom and less, again deeper, immediately four fathom then but three fathom, the sea going mightily and high. At last we recovered, God be thanked, in some despair, to sea room enough.

In this distress, we had vigilant eye unto the Admiral, whom we saw cast away, without power to give the men succour, neither could we espy any of the men that leaped overboard to save themselves, either in the same pinnace, or cock, or upon rafters, and such like means presenting themselves to men in those extremities, for we desired to save the men by every possible means. But all in vain, sith God had determined their ruin; yet all that day, and part of the next, we beat up and down as near unto the wrack as was possible for us, looking out if by good hap we might espy any of them.

This was a heavy and grievous event, to lose at one blow our chief ship freighted with great provision, gathered together with much travail, care, long time, and difficulty; but more was the loss of our men, which perished to the number almost of a hundred souls. Amongst whom was drowned a learned man, a Hungarian (Stephen Parmenius), born in the city of Buda, called thereof Budoeus, who, of piety and zeal to good attempts, adventured in this action, minding to record in the Latin tongue the gests and things worthy of remembrance, happening in this discovery, to the honour of our nations, the same being adorned with the eloquent style of this orator and rare poet of our time.

Here also perished our Saxon refiner and discoverer of inestimable riches, as it was left amongst some of us in undoubted hope. No less heavy was the loss of the captain, Maurice Browne, a virtuous, honest, and discreet gentleman, overseen only in liberty given late before to men that ought to have been restrained, who showed himself a man resolved, and never unprepared for death, as by his last act of this tragedy appeared, by report of them that escaped this wrack miraculously, as shall be hereafter declared. For when all hope was past of recovering the ship, and that men began to give over, and to save themselves, the captain was advised before to shift also for his life, by the pinnace at the stern of the ship; but refusing that counsel, he would not give example with the first to leave the ship, but used all means to exhort his people not to despair, nor so to leave off their labour, choosing rather to die than to incur infamy by forsaking his charge, which then might be thought to have perished through his default, showing an ill precedent unto his men, by leaving the ship first himself. With this mind he mounted upon the highest deck, where he attended imminent death, and unavoidable; how long, I leave it to God, who withdraweth not his comfort from his servants at such times.

In the mean season, certain, to the number of fourteen persons, leaped into a small pinnace, the bigness of a Thames barge, which was made in the Newfoundland, cut off the rope wherewith it was towed, and committed themselves to God's mercy, amidst the storm, and rage of sea and winds, destitute of food, not so much as a drop of fresh water. The boat seeming overcharged in foul weather with company, Edward Headly, a valiant soldier, and well reputed of his company, preferring the greater to the lesser, thought better that some of them perished than all, made this motion, to cast lots, and them to be thrown overboard upon whom the lots fell, thereby to lighten the boat, which otherways seemed impossible to live, and offered himself with the first, content to take his adventure gladly: which nevertheless Richard Clarke, that was master of the Admiral, and one of this number, refused, advising to abide God's pleasure, who was able to save all, as well as a few. The boat was carried before the wind, continuing six days and nights in the ocean, and arrived at last with the men, alive, but weak, upon the Newfoundland, saving that the foresaid Headly, who had been late sick, and another called of us Brazil, of his travel into those countries, died by the way, famished, and less able to hold out than those of better health. . . . Thus whom God delivered from drowning, he appointed to be famished; who doth give limits to man's times, and ordaineth the manner and circumstance of dying: whom, again, he will preserve, neither sea nor famine can confound. For those that arrived upon the Newfoundland were brought into France by certain Frenchmen, then being upon the coast.

After this heavy chance, we continued in beating the sea up and down, expecting when the weather would clear up that we might yet bear in with the land, which we judged not far off either the continent or some island. For we many times, and in sundry places found ground at 50, 45, 40 fathoms, and less. The ground coming upon our lead, being sometime cozy sand and other while a broad shell, with a little sand about it.

Our people lost courage daily after this ill success, the weather continuing thick and blustering, with increase of cold, winter drawing on, which took from them all hope of amendment, settling an assurance of worse weather to grow upon us every day. The leeside of us lay full of flats and dangers, inevitable if the wind blew hard at south. Some again doubted we were ingulfed in the Bay of St. Lawrence, the coast full of dangers, and unto us unknown. But above all, provision waxed scant, and hope of supply was gone with the loss of our Admiral. Those in the frigate were already pinched with spare allowance, and want of clothes chiefly: thereupon they besought the General to return to England before they all perished. And to them of the *Golden Hind* they made signs of distress, pointing to their mouths, and to their clothes thin and ragged: then immediately they also of the *Golden Hind* grew to be of the same opinion and desire to return home.

The former reasons having also moved the General to have compassion of his poor men, in whom he saw no want of good will, but of means fit to perform the action they came for, he resolved upon retire: and calling the captain and master of the *Hind*, he yielded them many reasons, enforcing this unexpected return, withal protesting himself greatly satisfied with that he had seen and knew already, reiterating these words: *Be content, we have seen enough, and take no care of expense past: I will set you forth royally the next spring, if God send us safe home. Therefore I pray you let us no longer strive here, where we fight against*

the elements. Omitting circumstance, how unwillingly the captain and master of the *Hind* condescended to this motion, his own company can testify; yet comforted with the General's promise of a speedy return at spring, and induced by other apparent reasons, proving an impossibility to accomplish the action at that time, it was concluded on all hands to retire.

So upon Saturday in the afternoon, the 31 of August, we changed our course, and returned back for England. At which very instant, even in winding about, there passed along between us and towards the land which we now forsook a very lion to our seeming, in shape, hair, and colour, not swimming after the manner of a beast by moving of his feet, but rather sliding upon the water with his whole body excepting the legs, in sight, neither yet diving under, and again rising above the water, as the manner is of whales, dolphins, tunnies, porpoises, and all other fish: but confidently showing himself above water without hiding: notwithstanding, we presented ourselves in open view and gesture to amaze him, as all creatures will be commonly at a sudden gaze and sight of men. Thus he passed along turning his head to and fro, yawing and gaping wide, with ugly demonstration of long teeth, and glaring eyes; and to bid us a farewell, coming right against the *Hind*, he sent forth a horrible voice, roaring or bellowing as doth a lion, which spectacle we all beheld so far as we were able to discern the same, as men prone to wonder at every strange thing, as this doubtless was, to see a lion in the ocean sea, or fish in shape of a lion. What opinion others had thereof, and chiefly the General himself, I forbear to deliver: but he took it for ***bonum omen***, rejoicing that he was in war against such an enemy, if it were the devil. The wind was large for England at our return, but very high, and the sea rough, insomuch as the frigate, wherein the General went, was almost swallowed up.

Monday in the afternoon we passed in sight of Cape Race, having made as much way in little more than two days and nights back again, as before we had done in eight days from Cape Race unto the place where our ship perished. Which hindrance thitherward, and speed back again, is to be imputed unto the swift current, as well as to the winds, which we had more large in our return. This Monday the General came aboard the *Hind*, to have the surgeon of the *Hind* to dress his foot, which he hurt by treading upon a nail: at which time we comforted each other with hope of hard success to be all past, and of the good to come. So agreeing to carry out lights always by night, that we might keep together, he departed into his frigate, being by no means to be entreated to tarry in the *Hind*, which had been more for his security. Immediately after followed a sharp storm, which we over passed for that time, praised be God.

The weather fair, the General came aboard the *Hind* again, to make merry together with the captain, master, and company, which was the last meeting, and continued there from morning until night. During which time there passed sundry discourses touching affairs past and to come, lamenting greatly the loss of his great ship, more of the men, but most of all his books and notes, and what else I know not, for which he was out of measure grieved, the same doubtless being some matter of more importance than his books, which I could not draw from him: yet by circumstance I gathered the same to be the ore which Daniel the Saxon had brought unto him in the Newfoundland. Whatsoever it was, the remembrance touched him so deep as, not able to contain himself, he beat his boy in great rage, even at the same time, so long after the miscarrying of the great ship, because upon a fair day, when we were becalmed upon the coast of the Newfoundland near unto Cape Race, he sent his boy aboard the Admiral to fetch certain things: amongst which, this being chief, was yet forgotten and left behind. After which time he could never conveniently send again aboard the great ship, much less he doubted her ruin so near at hand.

Herein my opinion was better confirmed diversely, and by sundry conjectures, which maketh me have the greater hope of this rich mine. For whereas the General had never before good conceit of these north parts of the world, now his mind was wholly fixed upon the Newfoundland. And as before he refused not to grant assignments liberally to them that required the same into these north parts, now he became contrarily affected, refusing to make any so large grants, especially of St. John's, which certain English merchants made suit for, offering to employ their money and travail upon the same yet neither by their own suit, nor of others of his own company, whom he seemed willing to pleasure, it could be obtained. Also laying down his determination in the spring following for disposing of his voyage then to be re-attempted: he assigned the captain and master of the *Golden Hind* unto the south discovery, and reserved unto himself the north, affirming that this voyage had won his heart from the south, and that he was now become a northern man altogether.

Last, being demanded what means he had, at his arrival in England, to compass the charges of so great preparation as he intended to make the next spring, having determined upon two fleets, one for the south, another for the north; *Leave that to me*, he replied, *I will ask a penny of no man. I will bring good tiding unto her Majesty, who will be so gracious to lend me 10,000 pounds*, willing us therefore to be of good cheer; for *he did thank God*, he said, *with all his heart for that he had seen, the same being enough for us all, and that we needed not to seek any further*. And these last words he would often repeat, with demonstration of great fervency of mind, being himself very confident and settled in belief of inestimable good by this voyage; which the greater number of his followers nevertheless mistrusted altogether, not being made partakers of those secrets, which the General kept unto himself. Yet all of them that are living may be witnesses of his words and protestations, which sparingly I have delivered.

Leaving the issue of this good hope unto God, who knoweth the truth only, and can at His good pleasure bring the same to light, I will hasten to the end of this tragedy, which must be knit up in the person of our General. And as it was God's ordinance upon him, even so the vehement persuasion and entreaty of his friends could nothing avail to divert him of a wilful resolution of going through in his frigate; which was overcharged upon the decks with fights, nettings, and small artillery, too cumbersome for so small a boat that was to pass through the ocean sea at that season of the year, when by course we might expect much storm of foul weather. Whereof, indeed, we had enough.

But when he was entreated by the captain, master, and other his well-willers of the *Hind* not to venture in the frigate, this was his answer: ***I will not forsake my little company going homeward, with whom I have passed so many storms and perils.*** And in very truth he was urged to be so over hard by hard reports given of him that he was afraid of the sea; albeit this was rather rashness than advised resolution, to prefer the wind of a vain report to the weight of his own life. Seeing he would not bend to reason, he had provision out of the *Hind*, such as was wanting aboard his frigate. And so we committed him to God's protection, and set him aboard his pinnace, we being more than 300 leagues onward of our way home.

By that time we had brought the Islands of Azores south of us; yet we then keeping much to the north, until we had got into the height and elevation of England, we met with very foul weather and terrible seas, breaking short and high, pyramid-wise. The reason whereof seemed to proceed either of hilly grounds high and low within the sea, as we see hills and vales upon the land, upon which the seas do mount and fall, or else the cause proceedeth of diversity of winds, shifting often in sundry points, all which having power to move the great ocean, which again is not presently settled, so many seas do encounter together, as there had been diversity of winds. Howsoever it cometh to pass, men which all their lifetime had occupied the sea never saw more outrageous seas, we had also upon our mainyard an apparition of a little fire by night, which seamen do call Castor and Pollux. But we had only one, which they take an evil sign of more tempest; the same is usual in storms.

Monday, the 9 of September, in the afternoon, the frigate was near cast away, oppressed by waves, yet at that time recovered; and giving forth signs of joy, the General, sitting abaft with a book in his hand, cried out to us in the *Hind*, so oft as we did approach within hearing, ***We are as near to heaven by sea as by land!*** Reiterating the same speech, well beseeming a soldier, resolute in Jesus Christ, as I can testify he was.

The same Monday night, about twelve of the clock, or not long after, the frigate being ahead of us in the *Golden Hind*, suddenly her lights were out, whereof as it were in a moment we lost the sight, and withal our watch cried ***the General was cast away***, which was too true. For in that moment the frigate was devoured and swallowed up of the sea. Yet still we looked out all that night, and ever after until we arrived upon the coast of England; omitting no small sail at sea, unto which we gave not the tokens between us agreed upon to have perfect knowledge of each other, if we should at any time be separated.

In great torment of weather and peril of drowning it pleased God to send safe home the *Golden Hind*, which arrived in Falmouth the 22 of September, being Sunday, not without as great danger escaped in a flaw coming from the south-east, with such thick mist that we could not discern land to put in right with the haven. From Falmouth we went to Dartmouth, and lay there at anchor before the Range, while the captain went aland to enquire if there had been any news of the frigate, which, sailing well, might happily have been before us; also to certify Sir John Gilbert, brother unto the General, of our hard success, whom the captain desired, while his men were yet aboard him, and were witnesses of all occurrences in that voyage, it might please him to take the examination of every person particularly, in discharge of his and their faithful endeavour. Sir John Gilbert refused so to do, holding himself satisfied with report made by the captain, and not altogether despairing of his brother's safety, offered friendship and courtesy to the captain and his company, requiring to have his bark brought into the harbour; in furtherance whereof a boat was sent to help to tow her in.

Nevertheless, when the captain returned aboard his ship, he found his men bent to depart every man to his home; and then the wind serving to proceed higher upon the coast, they demanded money to carry them home, some to London, others to Harwich, and elsewhere, if the barque should be carried into Dartmouth and they discharged so far from home, or else to take benefit of the wind, then serving to draw nearer home, which should be a less charge unto the captain, and great ease unto the men, having else far to go. Reason accompanied with necessity persuaded the captain, who sent his lawful excuse and cause of this sudden departure unto Sir John Gilbert, by the boat of Dartmouth, and from thence the *Golden Hind* departed and took harbour at Weymouth. All the men tired with the tediousness of so unprofitable a voyage to their seeming, in which their long expense of time, much toil and labour, hard diet, and continual hazard of life was unrecompensed; their captain nevertheless by his great charges impaired greatly thereby, yet comforted in the goodness of God, and His undoubted providence following him in all that voyage, as it doth always those at other times whosoever have confidence in Him alone. Yet have we more near feeling and perseverance of His powerful hand and protection when God doth bring us together with others into one same peril, in which He leaveth them and delivereth us, making us thereby the beholders, but not partakers, of their ruin. Even so, amongst very many difficulties, discontentments, mutinies, conspiracies, sicknesses, mortality, spoilings, and wracks by sea, which were afflictions more than in so small a fleet or so short a time may be supposed, albeit true in every particularity, as partly by the former relation may be collected, and some I suppressed with silence for their sakes living, it pleased God to support this company, of which only one man died of a malady inveterate, and long infested, the rest kept together in reasonable contentment and concord, beginning, continuing, and ending the voyage, which none else did accomplish, either not pleased with the action, or impatient of wants, or prevented by death.

Thus have I delivered the contents of the enterprise and last action of Sir Humfrey Gilbert, Knight, faithfully, for so much as I thought meet to be published; wherein may always appear, though he be extinguished, some sparks of his virtues, be remaining firm and resolute in a purpose by all pretence honest and godly, as was this, to discover, possess, and to reduce unto the service of God and Christian piety those remote and heathen countries of America not actually possessed by Christians, and most rightly appertaining unto the crown of England, unto the which as his zeal deserveth high commendation, even so he may justly be taxed of temerity, and presumption rather, in two respects. First, when yet there was only probability, not a certain and determinate place of habitation selected, neither any demonstration if commodity there *in esse*, to induce his followers; nevertheless, he both was too prodigal of his own patrimony and too careless of other men's expenses to employ both his and their substance upon a ground imagined good. The which falling, very like his associates were promised, and made it their best reckoning, to be salved some other way, which pleased not God to prosper in his first and great preparation. Secondly, when by his former preparation he was enfeebled of ability and credit to perform his designments, as it were impatient to abide in expectation better opportunity, and means which God might raise, he thrust himself again into the action, for which he was not fit, presuming the cause pretended on God's behalf would carry him to the desired end. Into which having thus made re-entry, he could not yield again to withdraw, though he saw no encouragement to proceed; lest his credit, foiled in his first attempt, in a second should utterly be disgraced. Between extremities he made a right adventure, putting all to God and good fortune; and, which was worst, refused not to entertain every person and means whatsoever, to furnish out this expedition, the success whereof hath been declared.

But such is the infinite bounty of God, who from every evil deriveth good. For besides that fruit may grow in time of our travelling into those north-west lands, the crosses, turmoils, and afflictions, both in the preparation and execution of this voyage, did correct the intemperate humours which before we noted to be in this gentleman, and made unsavoury and less delightful his other manifold virtues. Then as he was refined, and made nearer drawing unto the image of God so it pleased the Divine will to resume him unto Himself, whither both his and every other high and noble mind have always aspired.

www.bookjungle.com *email: sales@bookjungle.com fax: 630-214-0564 mail: Book Jungle PO Box 2226 Champaign, IL 61825*

The Codes Of Hammurabi And Moses
W. W. Davies

QTY

The discovery of the Hammurabi Code is one of the greatest achievements of archaeology, and is of paramount interest, not only to the student of the Bible, but also to all those interested in ancient history...

Religion **ISBN:** *1-59462-338-4* **Pages:**132 *MSRP $12.95*

The Theory of Moral Sentiments
Adam Smith

QTY

This work from 1749. contains original theories of conscience amd moral judgment and it is the foundation for systemof morals.

Philosophy **ISBN:** *1-59462-777-0* **Pages:**536 *MSRP $19.95*

Jessica's First Prayer
Hesba Stretton

QTY

In a screened and secluded corner of one of the many railway-bridges which span the streets of London there could be seen a few years ago, from five o'clock every morning until half past eight, a tidily set-out coffee-stall, consisting of a trestle and board, upon which stood two large tin cans, with a small fire of charcoal burning under each so as to keep the coffee boiling during the early hours of the morning when the work-people were thronging into the city on their way to their daily toil...

Childrens **ISBN:** *1-59462-373-2* **Pages:**84 *MSRP $9.95*

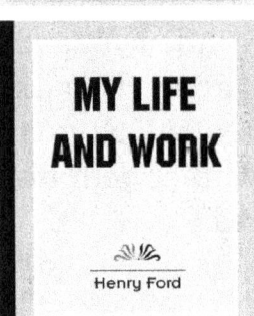

My Life and Work
Henry Ford

QTY

Henry Ford revolutionized the world with his implementation of mass production for the Model T automobile. Gain valuable business insight into his life and work with his own auto-biography... "We have only started on our development of our country we have not as yet, with all our talk of wonderful progress, done more than scratch the surface. The progress has been wonderful enough but..."

Biographies/ **ISBN:** *1-59462-198-5* **Pages:**300 *MSRP $21.95*

www.bookjungle.com email: sales@bookjungle.com fax: 630-214-0564 mail: Book Jungle PO Box 2226 Champaign, IL 61825

The Art of Cross-Examination
Francis Wellman

QTY

I presume it is the experience of every author, after his first book is published upon an important subject, to be almost overwhelmed with a wealth of ideas and illustrations which could readily have been included in his book, and which to his own mind, at least, seem to make a second edition inevitable. Such certainly was the case with me; and when the first edition had reached its sixth impression in five months, I rejoiced to learn that it seemed to my publishers that the book had met with a sufficiently favorable reception to justify a second and considerably enlarged edition. ..

Reference   ISBN: *1-59462-647-2*   Pages:412 MSRP *$19.95*

On the Duty of Civil Disobedience
Henry David Thoreau

QTY

Thoreau wrote his famous essay, On the Duty of Civil Disobedience, as a protest against an unjust but popular war and the immoral but popular institution of slave-owning. He did more than write—he declined to pay his taxes, and was hauled off to gaol in consequence. Who can say how much this refusal of his hastened the end of the war and of slavery ?

Law   ISBN: *1-59462-747-9*   Pages:48 MSRP *$7.45*

Dream Psychology Psychoanalysis for Beginners
Sigmund Freud

QTY

Sigmund Freud, born Sigismund Schlomo Freud (May 6, 1856 - September 23, 1939), was a Jewish-Austrian neurologist and psychiatrist who co-founded the psychoanalytic school of psychology. Freud is best known for his theories of the unconscious mind, especially involving the mechanism of repression; his redefinition of sexual desire as mobile and directed towards a wide variety of objects; and his therapeutic techniques, especially his understanding of transference in the therapeutic relationship and the presumed value of dreams as sources of insight into unconscious desires.

Psychology   ISBN: *1-59462-905-6*   Pages:196 MSRP *$15.45*

The Miracle of Right Thought
Orison Swett Marden

QTY

Believe with all of your heart that you will do what you were made to do. When the mind has once formed the habit of holding cheerful, happy, prosperous pictures, it will not be easy to form the opposite habit. It does not matter how improbable or how far away this realization may see, or how dark the prospects may be, if we visualize them as best we can, as vividly as possible, hold tenaciously to them and vigorously struggle to attain them, they will gradually become actualized, realized in the life. But a desire, a longing without endeavor, a yearning abandoned or held indifferently will vanish without realization.

Self Help   ISBN: *1-59462-644-8*   Pages:360 MSRP *$25.45*

www.bookjungle.com email: sales@bookjungle.com fax: 630-214-0564 mail: Book Jungle PO Box 2226 Champaign, IL 61825

QTY

	Title	ISBN	Price
☐	**The Rosicrucian Cosmo-Conception Mystic Christianity** by *Max Heindel*	ISBN: 1-59462-188-8	**$38.95**
	The Rosicrucian Cosmo-conception is not dogmatic, neither does it appeal to any other authority than the reason of the student. It is: not controversial, but is: sent forth in the, hope that it may help to clear...		New Age/Religion Pages 646
☐	**Abandonment To Divine Providence** by *Jean-Pierre de Caussade*	ISBN: 1-59462-228-0	**$25.95**
	"The Rev. Jean Pierre de Caussade was one of the most remarkable spiritual writers of the Society of Jesus in France in the 18th Century. His death took place at Toulouse in 1751. His works have gone through many editions and have been republished...		Inspirational/Religion Pages 400
☐	**Mental Chemistry** by *Charles Haanel*	ISBN: 1-59462-192-6	**$23.95**
	Mental Chemistry allows the change of material conditions by combining and appropriately utilizing the power of the mind. Much like applied chemistry creates something new and unique out of careful combinations of chemicals the mastery of mental chemistry...		New Age Pages 354
☐	**The Letters of Robert Browning and Elizabeth Barret Barrett 1845-1846 vol II** by *Robert Browning and Elizabeth Barrett*	ISBN: 1-59462-193-4	**$35.95**
			Biographies Pages 596
☐	**Gleanings In Genesis (volume I)** by *Arthur W. Pink*	ISBN: 1-59462-130-6	**$27.45**
	Appropriately has Genesis been termed "the seed plot of the Bible" for in it we have, in germ form, almost all of the great doctrines which are afterwards fully developed in the books of Scripture which follow...		Religion/Inspirational Pages 420
☐	**The Master Key** by *L. W. de Laurence*	ISBN: 1-59462-001-6	**$30.95**
	In no branch of human knowledge has there been a more lively increase of the spirit of research during the past few years than in the study of Psychology, Concentration and Mental Discipline. The requests for authentic lessons in Thought Control, Mental Discipline and...		New Age/Business Pages 422
☐	**The Lesser Key Of Solomon Goetia** by *L. W. de Laurence*	ISBN: 1-59462-092-X	**$9.95**
	This translation of the first book of the "Lernegton" which is now for the first time made accessible to students of Talismanic Magic was done, after careful collation and edition, from numerous Ancient Manuscripts in Hebrew, Latin, and French...		New Age/Occult Pages 92
☐	**Rubaiyat Of Omar Khayyam** by *Edward Fitzgerald*	ISBN: 1-59462-332-5	**$13.95**
	Edward Fitzgerald, whom the world has already learned, in spite of his own efforts to remain within the shadow of anonymity, to look upon as one of the rarest poets of the century, was born at Bredfield, in Suffolk, on the 31st of March, 1809. He was the third son of John Purcell...		Music Pages 172
☐	**Ancient Law** by *Henry Maine*	ISBN: 1-59462-128-4	**$29.95**
	The chief object of the following pages is to indicate some of the earliest ideas of mankind, as they are reflected in Ancient Law, and to point out the relation of those ideas to modern thought.		Religiom/History Pages 452
☐	**Far-Away Stories** by *William J. Locke*	ISBN: 1-59462-129-2	**$19.45**
	"Good wine needs no bush, but a collection of mixed vintages does. And this book is just such a collection. Some of the stories I do not want to remain buried for ever in the museum files of dead magazine-numbers an author's not unpardonable vanity..."		Fiction Pages 272
☐	**Life of David Crockett** by *David Crockett*	ISBN: 1-59462-250-7	**$27.45**
	"Colonel David Crockett was one of the most remarkable men of the times in which he lived. Born in humble life, but gifted with a strong will, an indomitable courage, and unremitting perseverance...		Biographies/New Age Pages 424
☐	**Lip-Reading** by *Edward Nitchie*	ISBN: 1-59462-206-X	**$25.95**
	Edward B. Nitchie, founder of the New York School for the Hard of Hearing, now the Nitchie School of Lip-Reading, Inc, wrote "LIP-READING Principles and Practice". The development and perfecting of this meritorious work on lip-reading was an undertaking...		How-to Pages 400
☐	**A Handbook of Suggestive Therapeutics, Applied Hypnotism, Psychic Science** by *Henry Munro*	ISBN: 1-59462-214-0	**$24.95**
			Health/New Age/Health/Self-help Pages 376
☐	**A Doll's House: and Two Other Plays** by *Henrik Ibsen*	ISBN: 1-59462-112-8	**$19.95**
	Henrik Ibsen created this classic when in revolutionary 1848 Rome. Introducing some striking concepts in playwriting for the realist genre, this play has been studied the world over.		Fiction/Classics/Plays 308
☐	**The Light of Asia** by *sir Edwin Arnold*	ISBN: 1-59462-204-3	**$13.95**
	In this poetic masterpiece, Edwin Arnold describes the life and teachings of Buddha. The man who was to become known as Buddha to the world was born as Prince Gautama of India but he rejected the worldly riches and abandoned the reigns of power when...		Religion/History/Biographies Pages 170
☐	**The Complete Works of Guy de Maupassant** by *Guy de Maupassant*	ISBN: 1-59462-157-8	**$16.95**
	"For days and days, nights and nights, I had dreamed of that first kiss which was to consecrate our engagement, and I knew not on what spot I should put my lips..."		Fiction/Classics Pages 240
☐	**The Art of Cross-Examination** by *Francis L. Wellman*	ISBN: 1-59462-309-0	**$26.95**
	Written by a renowned trial lawyer, Wellman imparts his experience and uses case studies to explain how to use psychology to extract desired information through questioning.		How-to/Science/Reference Pages 408
☐	**Answered or Unanswered?** by *Louisa Vaughan*	ISBN: 1-59462-248-5	**$10.95**
	Miracles of Faith in China		Religion Pages 112
☐	**The Edinburgh Lectures on Mental Science (1909)** by *Thomas*	ISBN: 1-59462-008-3	**$11.95**
	This book contains the substance of a course of lectures recently given by the writer in the Queen Street Hall, Edinburgh. Its purpose is to indicate the Natural Principles governing the relation between Mental Action and Material Conditions...		New Age/Psychology Pages 148
☐	**Ayesha** by *H. Rider Haggard*	ISBN: 1-59462-301-5	**$24.95**
	Verily and indeed it is the unexpected that happens! Probably if there was one person upon the earth from whom the Editor of this, and of a certain previous history, did not expect to hear again...		Classics Pages 380
☐	**Ayala's Angel** by *Anthony Trollope*	ISBN: 1-59462-352-X	**$29.95**
	The two girls were both pretty, but Lucy who was twenty-one who supposed to be simple and comparatively unattractive, whereas Ayala was credited, as her Bombwhat romantic name might show, with poetic charm and a taste for romance. Ayala when her father died was nineteen...		Fiction Pages 484
☐	**The American Commonwealth** by *James Bryce*	ISBN: 1-59462-286-8	**$34.45**
	An interpretation of American democratic political theory. It examines political mechanics and society from the perspective of Scotsman James Bryce		Politics Pages 572
☐	**Stories of the Pilgrims** by *Margaret P. Pumphrey*	ISBN: 1-59462-116-0	**$17.95**
	This book explores pilgrims religious oppression in England as well as their escape to Holland and eventual crossing to America on the Mayflower, and their early days in New England...		History Pages 268

www.bookjungle.com email: sales@bookjungle.com fax: 630-214-0564 mail: Book Jungle PO Box 2226 Champaign, IL 61825

Title	ISBN	Price	QTY
The Fasting Cure by *Sinclair Upton* — In the Cosmopolitan Magazine for May, 1910, and in the Contemporary Review (London) for April, 1910, I published an article dealing with my experiences in fasting. I have written a great many magazine articles, but never one which attracted so much attention... *New Age/Self Help/Health Pages 164*	1-59462-222-1	$13.95	
Hebrew Astrology by *Sepharial* — In these days of advanced thinking it is a matter of common observation that we have left many of the old landmarks behind and that we are now pressing forward to greater heights and to a wider horizon than that which represented the mind-content of our progenitors... *Astrology Pages 144*	1-59462-308-2	$13.45	
Thought Vibration or The Law of Attraction in the Thought World by *William Walker Atkinson* — *Psychology/Religion Pages 144*	1-59462-127-6	$12.95	
Optimism by *Helen Keller* — Helen Keller was blind, deaf, and mute since 19 months old, yet famously learned how to overcome these handicaps, communicate with the world, and spread her lectures promoting optimism. An inspiring read for everyone... *Biographies/Inspirational Pages 84*	1-59462-108-X	$15.95	
Sara Crewe by *Frances Burnett* — In the first place, Miss Minchin lived in London. Her home was a large, dull, tall one, in a large, dull square, where all the houses were alike, and all the sparrows were alike, and where all the door-knockers made the same heavy sound... *Childrens/Classic Pages 88*	1-59462-360-0	$9.45	
The Autobiography of Benjamin Franklin by *Benjamin Franklin* — The Autobiography of Benjamin Franklin has probably been more extensively read than any other American historical work, and no other book of its kind has had such ups and downs of fortune. Franklin lived for many years in England, where he was agent... *Biographies/History Pages 332*	1-59462-135-7	$24.95	

Name	
Email	
Telephone	
Address	
City, State ZIP	

☐ Credit Card   ☐ Check / Money Order

Credit Card Number	
Expiration Date	
Signature	

Please Mail to: Book Jungle
PO Box 2226
Champaign, IL 61825
or Fax to: 630-214-0564

ORDERING INFORMATION

web: *www.bookjungle.com*
email: *sales@bookjungle.com*
fax: *630-214-0564*
mail: *Book Jungle PO Box 2226 Champaign, IL 61825*
or PayPal *to sales@bookjungle.com*

Please contact us for bulk discounts

DIRECT-ORDER TERMS

20% Discount if You Order Two or More Books
Free Domestic Shipping!
Accepted: Master Card, Visa, Discover, American Express

www.ingramcontent.com/pod-product-compliance
Lightning Source LLC
Chambersburg PA
CBHW081329040426
42453CB00013B/2354